JIGGERS & DRAMS

WHISKY JOURNAL

JIGGERS
& DRAMS
WHISKY JOURNAL

CARLO DEVITO

ROCK
POINT

Quarto is the authority on a wide range of topics.

Quarto educates, entertains and enriches the lives of
our readers—enthusiasts and lovers of hands-on living.

www.quartoknows.com

First published in the United States of America in 2016 by
Rock Point, a member of
Quarto Publishing Group USA Inc.
142 West 36th Street, 4th Floor
New York, New York 10018
quartoknows.com

Visit our blogs at quartoknows.com

10 9 8 7 6 5 4 3 2 1

ISBN: 978-1-63106-180-6

Cover Design: Heidi North
Interior Design: Marc J Cohen
Photo credits: Shutterstock

Printed in China

MIX
Paper from
responsible sources
FSC® C016973
www.fsc.org

CONTENTS

INTRODUCTION

There are two questions grain spirits editors are most often asked: What's the difference between the different types of whiskies, and which one's the best? The answer to the former is that it's complicated, but not that complicated. The answer to the latter is that the best one is the one you like! In this journal and guide, I'm going to break down the not-so-complicated differences between whiskies, bourbons, ryes, and everything in-between. Then I'm going to step back and allow you to discover your best whiskies, by giving you a framework to record your whisky experiences.

Whisky or Whiskey?

"The United States and Great Britain are two countries separated by a common language," is an often-quoted quip that's applicable to whisky, too. Many people in the United States and Ireland spell it "whiskey," but in this guide, when I'm referring to whisky generally, I'll stick with the "whisky" spelling that's prevalent throughout the rest of the world, including in the UK and by many leading US whisky distributors.

I've been fortunate to have experienced everything from high-end single malts to aged bourbons to newly made ryes. There's a new craft distilling movement brewing, and there's truly never been a better time to taste unique spirits. Just remember: there are two very important components to drinking whisky that this guide can't teach you—how you drink it and who you drink it with. Nothing accentuates good whisky better than being in a good cocktail, and nothing makes a sipper satisfying like a hearty, delicious meal to precede it. And nothing enhances food and drink better than enjoying them with family and friends.

That's why this journal is a little different than most, which have you just record your tasting notes. Much like a photo album or keepsake box, this journal will help store your memories of good whisky, good food, and good memories. Not only is there plenty of space for tasting notes, there's a section where you can paste down some label art, lines for you to record your thoughts and memories, and much more.

Don't feel like the long, involved stuff? After the long entry pages and your home bar stock list, there are some short entry pages, where you can get in, write down your quick thoughts, and get out. After the short and long whisky journal entries, you'll find a PERSONAL BUYING GUIDE, so you can record your favorite producers, styles, and food-and-whiskey pairings. And if you ever get lost, there's a glossary at the end.

But first, here's a brief history of America's favorite liquor.

WHISKY
HISTORY

III

WHISKY'S EARLY ORIGINS

The word whisky (or "whiskey," the preferred spelling by many Americans and the Irish) is a shortened version of the eighteenth century Irish-Scottish word whiskybae, itself a variant of the word usquebaugh, which was a conglomeration of uisge beatha (literally, "water of life"), a phrase that was used as early as the sixteenth century to describe the delicious spirit we know today.

But whisky was around even earlier than that. Many historians believe it was developed by medieval Irish monks who learned the skill of distillation from Middle Eastern perfume traders. Considered a valuable medicine that cured just about everything from lisps to wrinkles to smallpox, "water of life" became such a cure-all that the Irish proverb "What whisky does not cure cannot be cured" was born.

Soon, however, it became apparent that whisky had a different, more fun use. The Irish were drinking whisky to celebrate, as proven by an account in a book of early Irish history. The text, written in 1405, recounted the tragic story of a Gaelic nobleman who died from drinking too much whisky on Christmas Day.

Irish whisky continued to be made by monks until the infamous Dissolution of the Monasteries by power-hungry King Henry VIII. After that, whisky was made at home, a tradition of moonshine that has been reborn in many of today's small-batch craft whiskies. Back in those days, whisky was un-aged and undiluted, making it very raw and very high in alcohol. It wasn't the smooth, seductive caramel-colored liquor it is today.

Eventually, the first license to make whisky commercially was given to Sir Thomas Philips of Bushmills, Northern Ireland. The oldest licensed whisky distillery in the world, Bushmills still makes some of the finest aged whisky money can buy.

WHISKY IN THE US

When whisky came to America, it had to compete with a thriving rum trade, but the American Revolution brought an influx of Irish and Scottish immigrants as well as a British molasses blockade (necessary for the making of rum), and so American-made whisky was born.

In America, rye and corn grew better than barley—what had been traditionally used to make whisky in Ireland and Great Britain. The distinctive spicy taste of rye whisky perfectly fit the palates of the upper-class Virginias, who loved this new, American-made concoction. Even George Washington got in on the act, thanks to his Scottish plantation manager who had his slaves plant field after field of rye so that they could produce whiskey to drink, sell, and trade. Eventually, George Washington would have the largest whisky distillery in the United States, producing 11,000 gallons of whisky with five stills and a boiler.

George Washington made whisky that was 60 percent twice-distilled rye, 35 percent corn, and 5 percent barley. In 2007, his distillery was recreated at his historic Mt. Vernon home, and it produces a small batch of George Washington Whiskey each year.

Meanwhile, whisky continued to be a popular drink to make privately in one's home. By spending the time to ferment their rye and corn, farmers could get more money for their crops, transport it more easily (since it couldn't spoil), and have some liquor left over for special occasions.

Whisky had a big benefit to sellers other than being easy to make and being the patriotic drink-of-the-moment. Since they were able to produce it locally, there was no import tax on whisky, unlike just about every other spirit. So when Alexander Hamilton (then Secretary of the Treasury) decided to tax domestically produced liquor to help repay the United States' debts from the Revolutionary War, whisky producers weren't happy. Small farms, especially, were incensed that the tax unduly burdened the poor, since the rich distillery owners could easily handle the cost of the new tax.

Whisky producers in western Pennsylvania rose up in what became known as the Whiskey Rebellion. In July 1794, more than 500 Whiskey Boys (as they called themselves) attacked the homes of tax collectors in Pittsburgh. In a test of the new nation's ability to stop an armed uprising, President George Washington sent in the militia, who quickly dispersed the rebels. However, the tax proved hard to enforce, and Thomas Jefferson's administration would later repeal it.

Meanwhile, in the part of the Virginia colony that would become Kentucky, sweet whiskies made with mostly corn were starting to become common. Distributors poured this new whisky into oak barrels and sent it down the Mississippi River to New Orleans. On its months-long journey, it took on the rich color and mellow flavor of the oak wood, giving it an even more distinctive taste from traditional American whiskies. The barrels were stamped with their origin, and the ones from Bourbon County became especially well-known.

Whisky was well on its way to being America's most-loved, most-consumed beverage—in a time where clean drinking water was often hard for the common landowner to find, home-distilled whiskey was not, and it was even recommended by doctors for a whole host of ailments, not unlike their Irish monk forefathers.

Only in 1862, when (yet again) a tax on liquor was excised to help pay war debts (this time from the Civil War), did whiskey begin to descend the charts as the US's most-drunk beverage. Still, it was so popular that the "Bottled in Bond" Act of 1897 was imposed to strictly define what whisky was so it could be properly regulated. The argument continued well into the twentieth century, with President Taft finally settling the matter personally in 1909. After reportedly spending more than six months listening to the arguments of impassioned whisky producers, the president and future Supreme Court justice handed down his decision that "straight whisky" was whiskey with nothing but water added. Anything else would be known as "blended whisky" or worse, "imitation whisky." These legal and cultural rules for what constitutes true whisky still stand today.

WHISKY DURING PROHIBITION

In 1920, most of America's estimated 1,300 beer manufacturers shut down as the new Prohibition laws went into effect. Yet because of its believed medicinal value and its cultural significance in America, the Prohibition Act included a provision that allowed people to obtain a prescription for medicinal whiskey, up to one pint every ten days, from doctors, dentists, and even veterinarians. Although still produced in much more limited forms than before Prohibition, whisky was again the most widely available form of alcohol. While some purchased their whisky at Walgreens, others sought it out at speakeasies, and its production moved back to its underground roots, where unique, complex blends were personally bottled, labeled, and sold on the black market.

After Prohibition was repealed, American distilleries could once again freely produce whisky for all. But they never lost the culture of rules and regulations, and instead they grew to include the way the drink could be packaged and sold. Soon, whisky labels as well as family lineages of whisky producers became important, giving even more written and visual history to this culturally rich drink.

Today, whisky is as American as apple pie, even though Scotland and Ireland are known for the drink as well. In fact, Canada, Japan, and even India have their own special brand of whiskies, born of their own histories. As historic as it is beloved, I imagine some of us have our own personal histories that are intertwined with whisky, as well.

Whisky for Sale

Buying recreational alcohol at the pharmacist's counter was so commonplace during Prohibition that it worked its way into one of the era's most famous books, *The Great Gatsby*. As Daniel Okrent points out in his book *Last Call: The Rise and Fall of Prohibition*, when Daisy Buchanan describes Jay Gatsby as having built up "some drugstores, a lot of drugstores," she's actually saying he's a bootlegger.

HOW WHISKY IS MADE

Before we get into the different types of whiskies, here's a quick primer on how whisky is made. Once the barley (and sometimes, rye) is harvested, it's malted, which is the name for the process of soaking the grain and then laying it out to dry. This allows it to germinate, and its starches to more easily convert to sugars.

Beer: Whisky that Wasn't

Since beer and whisky are both made with grain, it's not surprising that the beginning processes of malting and mashing are practically identical. In fact, according to the American Distilling Institute, "To distill whisky you first have to make beer. Beer is a technical term for whisky wash." One wash goes into the distiller, and the other goes on to be brewed. No wonder they taste so great when they're reunited side-by-side at a bar.

Once the grains have been malted and ground down, they're added to any unmalted grains and water to form what's known as the mash. Since the water is almost always from a local source, its flavor and acidity can affect the whisky's character (for instance, some people say you can taste the limestone-enriched water in a true Kentucky bourbon). The mash is heated and stirred until much of its sugars are dissolved, then a small amount of yeast is added so that it begins fermenting.

Fermenting only takes a couple of days, a millisecond in the life of most aged whiskies, but many distilleries allow it to sit for longer to further develop their desired flavor. Now called "wash," it's then added to a still one batch at a time and then poured into oak barrels, where it matures for anywhere from a few years to a few decades.

Other than barely, distilled in a pot still rather than a column still, and aged in oak for at least three years (though most producers do it for

much, much longer). The care put into single malt Scotch shows—considered the best whisky in all of Scotland (and many would say, the world), it has a deep, pronounced flavor that might make you fall in love.

TYPES OF WHISKY

Most whiskies are made by the process I've just described, but there are a lot of variations that can make them different, from how many times it's been distilled to what kind of cask its aged in. Here are the basic definitions for different kinds of whiskies so that you have a general idea of what you're getting into before you sip!

Whisky (or Whiskey): Whisky is the general term for the distilled, alcoholic beverage made from fermented grain mash—some combination of barley, corn, rye, and wheat—and typically aged in wooden casks (most commonly, charred white oak).

Single Malt Whisky: Single malt whisky, as its name would suggest, is a whisky made from malted grains that come from a single distillery.

Grain Whisky: Like many whisky terms, "grain whisky" has a few different meanings. Scotch makers will refer to any whisky that's been made with a combination of grains and then aged in oak as "grain whisky" and whisky made from malted barley only as "malt whisky." In Scotland, the two are often blended together (making blended whisky). However, in the United Stated, grain whisky is often aged on its own (usually for a decade or more), and released as "single grain whiskey" even though it can contain any number of grains.

Blended Whisky: Blended whisky is a whisky made from two or more different kinds of mash, usually from different distilleries. Oftentimes, this is as seen as "stretching out" high-quality aged whisky with the less-expensive grain whiskies, but there are also many premium brands that use blends to expertly balance the flavors of different mashes, giving them a full, well-rounded flavor; for instance, the lightness of grain whisky can balance out the deep flavors of a single malt.

Scotch Whisky: Often simply called Scotch, this whisky was traditionally made in Scotland with malted barley in a accordance with Scottish law. However, American distributors have begun using the term to describe whisky that has been made in the USA, causing a bit of head-scratching over the nomenclature. Because Scotch is often blended from a variety of different mashes from different distilleries, it can have wildly different tastes, from fruity to smoky to everything in between.

Single Malt Scotch: This impressive whisky is made in Scotland from a single distillery. And indeed, "single distillery Scotch" might be a more apt name, as not all single malt scotches contain only grain that has been malted (although many do). Scotland takes single malt Scotch very seriously, and to earn the appellation on the label, the whisky must not only be made in Scotland, but with no grain other than barley, distilled in a pot still rather than a column still, and aged in oak for at least three years (though most producers do it for much, much longer). The care put into single malt Scotch shows—considered the best whisky in all of Scotland (and many would say, the world), it has a deep, pronounced flavor that might make you fall in love.

Bourbon: For every ardent Scotch lover you'll find an equally passionate bourbon lover, and in America, probably two. Bourbon is an American whisky made from mostly corn, and legally must be aged in charred oak, contain at least 51 percent corn, and be at least 80 proof. Because of the charred oak casks, bourbon has a distinctive woody flavor, and thanks to its corn it's usually one of the sweeter whiskeys. "Straight bourbon" is an American legal term for bourbon aged at least two years.

Rye Whisky: Like bourbon, this whisky made with at least 51 percent rye is an American invention. Less sweet than bourbon, this spicy whisky smoothes out as it ages and tends to be lighter than other whiskies, though it can still pack a punch.

Corn Whisky: Also known as unaged whisky, moonshine, or white whisky, this recent star of the craft cocktail scene is the base spirit most bourbons are made from before they've been aged. Drinkers love it because its full of character and each distillery's take on it can be completely unique. Meanwhile, distillers like it because it can be made and sold in a much shorter timeframe than aged whisky!

Canadian Whisky: Whisky made in Canada has a lot of variations, the most predominant being blended whiskies containing mostly corn or rye. Recently, Canadian whiskies have won a lot of fans in the US and abroad thanks to their light, smooth taste.

Irish Whiskey: Whisky made in Ireland varies from its Scottish cousin in more ways than being spelled with an "e." While Scotch whisky is only distilled twice, Irish whiskey is distilled three times. But more importantly, the Scottish use peat to power the kilns that dry the barley while it's being malted, while the Irish do not. This gives it a smoother finish and a less earthy taste than Scotch.

Indian Whisky: Believe it or not, the best-selling whisky in the world (called Officer's Choice) is from India. These likeable whiskies are usually blends (sometimes even incorporating whiskies from other countries) and are often made from fermented molasses, making them the sweetest whiskies on the market.

III

TASTING
WHISKY

The first thing you'll need when tasting whisky is a proper glass. But I'm not talking about the normal, short "rocks glass" you're probably used to drinking it in at a bar. A real whisky tasting glass has more in common with a champagne flute with a short stem. That's because to appreciate the nuance in a whisky, you need a tasting vessel that funnels the bouquet (or aroma) of the whisky up so it's focused around your nose, where it can be appreciated.

Is it absolutely necessary to have one of these glasses? No. But if you don't, go with a small wine glass rather than one of the lovely cocktail glasses you have in your cupboard.

Here's a way to see if you've chosen a glass that properly intensifies the whisky's smell. Get a nice aromatic cheese and cut a piece into a cube the size of a die. Take a sniff, then throw the cheese cube into the empty glass and put one hand over the top, sealing it with one hand while you swirl the glass with the other. Shake it up and down. Knock that cube around good! Stop. Lift your hand off and smell what's in the glass. It should be an amazing sensation far beyond that of when you simply smelled the cheese out in the open. A good glass makes good whisky smell even better. And just as a simmering pot of delicious food draws you in and makes you want to eat it, a good whisky will make you want to drink it.

Just Say No to Rocks

You should never add ice to your glass when you taste a whisky for the first time. The cold reduces the flavor profile, and waters down the whisky too much.

Once you have your glass ready, it's time to go through the five easy steps of tasting.

Step 1 : LOOK

Why do we look at whisky? Have you ever eaten anything—a hamburger, a steak, some lobster—without looking at it first? When you're in a restaurant and the waiter sets down a dish at a neighboring table, haven't you ever asked, "Hey, what is that?" Looking at food is an absolutely essential part of the dining experience, just as looking at whisky is essential to tasting it.

So what are you looking for when you look at whisky? Note what color the whisky is, and also its clarity. A whisky's color can range anywhere from pale straw to gold to a barky burnt amber. Usually the older the whisky the darker the color, but that isn't always true. (Bourbons tend to be the darkest.) It's also important to remember that caramel coloring is sometimes added to whisky to improve its desirability. Don't be fooled! The younger ones are usually color-corrected to make them look like their older counterparts.

Step 2: SWIRL

To taste whisky, pour only a small amount in your glass—if you fill it too much you won't be able to properly swirl it, which aerates it. Aerating, or adding oxygen to whisky, enhances its inherent aromas and allows its nose to more fully develop.

The best way to learn to swirl is to leave the glass on the table while moving its base in a circular motion. The whisky should swirl easily— two or three times usually does it. The idea is to coat the sides of the glass with the liquid. When the whisky settles back down into the bowl of the glass, the sides with be coated in rivulets of whisky descending downward. These are known as the legs, and the thickness of the traces they leave on the glass is the whisky's viscosity. Viscosity usually indicates glycerin, sugar, and alcohol content. Whiskies with more viscosity have more pronounced legs and a slower drip. They taste more robust, or chewier. Now it's time to take a sniff!

Step 3: SMELL

Have you ever walked into a home where someone has been roasting a chicken, or baking a pie? Doesn't it just absolutely make you drool? How about when you walk into a barbecue restaurant and smell the thick aroma of slow-cooked meat in succulent sauce? For the same reason we savor these smells, we savor the smell of whisky. Like any other part of the food experience, smell is an important part of eating: It not only adds to our overall enjoyment of the meal, but enhances the taste of the food itself.

What kinds of scents are we searching for when we smell whisky? Good and bad things. Good things include fruit smells like ripe apple and pear, cereal, grass, wood, floral scents, smoke, and maple syrup. Aromas that are bad to smell in whisky include mushroom, dank basement, and dirty sweatsock-like odors.

Step 4: SIP

When I say sip, I mean sip. Not gulp. The idea is to really try to taste the whisky and ask yourself what flavors and feelings you can discern. What should you be tasting for? Here are a few important questions to ask yourself:

- Is the whisky sweet or dry? Bourbons tend to be on the sweet side, while single malts tend to be on the drier side (but there's no hard-and-fast rule).

- Is it harsh or smooth as you roll it around your mouth? How intense is the experience? Some people like a bracing shot of whisky. Others prefer a smoother experience. Because whisky is usually 80 proof or more, you can tell a lot about the production and handling of the liquid just by how it tastes.

- What's its finish like? What flavors do you detect at the end of your sip? Spices like pepper, fennel, clove, or allspice? Other foods like shortbread or fruitcake? (For more possible flavors you might run into, see pages 20-21.) What are the flavors remaining in your mouth 15, 30, and 45 seconds later? Do they disappear, or linger?

- What mouth-feel you are experiencing? Is the whisky thick or thin? Is it a bit chewy, or does it go down easily?

Step 5: SAVOR

Let the experience of sipping whisky linger. Take your time, and get ready for the next swig. This time, you are going to add water. Yes! You're going to add just a little bit. A small splash of water is perfect to take down the alcohol a drop and get those flavors and aromas going, akin to letting wine breathe, but even more so.

Look, swirl, smell, and sip all over again now that there's a little water in it. In some cases your impressions might stay the same. But oftentimes, water makes a world of difference.

What the Dickens?

Who knew *The Christmas Carol* had its roots in whisky? The real Ebenezer Scrooge (the basis for Dickens' character in the story) was a successful grain merchant and distiller in the UK. Unlike the fictional character, the real Ebenezer was a party animal who loved the ladies.

WHISKY WORDS

When you read reviews about whisky, you'll find all kinds of fruits, cereals, woods, spices, and other flavors to describe it. No, there is no banana or leather actually in the whisky. But whisky can have flavors that remind you of those things. Here are some common words people use to describe the way whisky smells and tastes:

Baked goods: Bread (or yeast extract), biscuits, shortbread, waffles, corn muffins, oatmeal cookies

Barnyard: Leather, hayloft, dried grass, stones, sweat

Botanicals: Juniper, coriander, basil, rosemary, thyme, sage, lemongrass, mint

Cereals: Corn, oatmeal, barley, rye, linseed, malt, flour, cornflakes

Chemicals: Turpentine, paint, varnish, menthol, plastic, wax

Flowers: Elderflower, orange blossoms, roses, violets, carnations, honeysuckle, lavender, dried flowers

Fruit (berries): Grapes, strawberries, raspberries, red currants, black currants, blackberries

Fruit (citrus): Orange, tangerine, grapefruit, lemon, lime

Fruit (dried): Figs, dates, prunes, raisins, sultana, citrus peel, fruitcake, mincemeat

Fruit (stone): Apples, gooseberries, pears, apricots, peaches, plums, red cherries, black cherries, nectarines

Fruit (tropical): Bananas, kiwi, lychees, mangos, melons, passionfruit, pineapple

Herbaceous:	Grass, hay, eucalyptus, black currant leaf, heather, hemp, tobacco
Nutty:	Almonds, chocolate, hazelnuts, coconut, walnuts, pecans
Off flavors:	Rubber, spent matches, boiled cabbage, drains, mushrooms, shoe polish, dank basement, sulfur, hard-boiled eggs
Other alcohol:	Amaretto, sherry, port
Other food or drink:	Toast, coffee, meatiness, gravy, cheese
Peat:	Forest floor, peaty, mossy, earthy, smoky, seaweed
Spices:	Allspice, anise, fennel, liquorish, cinnamon, cloves, ginger, nutmeg, black pepper, white pepper
Sweetness:	Vanilla, butterscotch, caramel, burnt sugar, toffee, molasses, maple syrup, custard, candied fruits, vegemite
Vegetables:	Bell pepper, mushroom, asparagus
Wood:	Cedar, char, sawdust

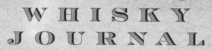

WHISKY JOURNAL

Certain whiskies are just special, but you already know this. Some are special because the whisky was deliciously smooth yet smoky in the perfect way; and sometimes it's because the meal you had before it was fantastic, the conversation was sparkling, and the setting was unique. Most likely it was the combination.

This section is a place to help you remember all those things—what the whisky tasted like, and why it tasted so great. In addition to writing down your tasting notes including color, aroma, taste, and mouth-feel; write down whom you enjoyed the whisky with, what food you ate, or anything else that added to the special vibe of the experience. There's space to paste a label, but you might want to paste a photograph, cigar band, menu, or cocktail-napkin drawing instead! Feel free to draw, write, highlight, scribble, or clip. Do anything you need to make the page as memorable as possible.

NAME

PRODUCER | AGE

TYPE (bourbon, single malt Scotch, etc.) | GRAINS

☐ CORN   ☐ RYE

DESCRIPTIONS

COLOR | AROMA

TASTE | MOUTH-FEEL

TEXTURE

BALANCE

LENGTH

WHEN?

WHERE?

WHO WITH?

FOOD & COCKTAIL PAIRINGS

WITH WATER?

☐ YES ☐ NO

WITH ICE?

☐ YES ☐ NO

LABEL/NOTES

NAME

PRODUCER

AGE

TYPE (bourbon, single malt Scotch, etc.)

GRAINS

☐ CORN   ☐ RYE

DESCRIPTIONS

COLOR

AROMA

TASTE

MOUTH-FEEL

TEXTURE

BALANCE

LENGTH

WHEN?

WHERE?

WHO WITH?

FOOD & COCKTAIL PAIRINGS

WITH WATER?

☐ YES   ☐ NO

WITH ICE?

☐ YES   ☐ NO

LABEL/NOTES

NAME

PRODUCER	AGE

TYPE (bourbon, single malt Scotch, etc.)	GRAINS
	□ CORN □ RYE

DESCRIPTIONS

COLOR	AROMA

TASTE	MOUTH-FEEL

TEXTURE

BALANCE

LENGTH

WHEN?

WHERE?

WHO WITH?

FOOD & COCKTAIL PAIRINGS

WITH WATER?

☐ YES   ☐ NO

WITH ICE?

☐ YES   ☐ NO

LABEL/NOTES

NAME

PRODUCER | AGE

TYPE (bourbon, single malt Scotch, etc.) | GRAINS

☐ CORN   ☐ RYE

DESCRIPTIONS

COLOR | AROMA

TASTE | MOUTH-FEEL

TEXTURE

BALANCE

LENGTH

When?

Where?

Who with?

FOOD & COCKTAIL PAIRINGS

With water?

☐ Yes   ☐ No

With ice?

☐ Yes   ☐ No

Label/Notes

NAME

PRODUCER | AGE

TYPE (bourbon, single malt Scotch, etc.) | GRAINS

☐ CORN ☐ RYE

DESCRIPTIONS

COLOR | AROMA

TASTE | MOUTH-FEEL

TEXTURE

BALANCE

LENGTH

WHEN?

WHERE?

WHO WITH?

FOOD & COCKTAIL PAIRINGS

WITH WATER?

☐ YES   ☐ NO

WITH ICE?

☐ YES   ☐ NO

LABEL/NOTES

NAME

PRODUCER | AGE

TYPE (bourbon, single malt Scotch, etc.) | GRAINS
| □ CORN □ RYE

DESCRIPTIONS

COLOR | AROMA

TASTE | MOUTH-FEEL

TEXTURE

BALANCE

LENGTH

WHEN?

WHERE?

WHO WITH?

FOOD & COCKTAIL PAIRINGS

WITH WATER?

☐ YES   ☐ NO

WITH ICE?

☐ YES   ☐ NO

LABEL/NOTES

NAME

PRODUCER	AGE

TYPE (bourbon, single malt Scotch, etc.)	GRAINS
	☐ CORN ☐ RYE

DESCRIPTIONS

COLOR	AROMA

TASTE	MOUTH-FEEL

TEXTURE

BALANCE

LENGTH

WHEN?

WHERE?

WHO WITH?

FOOD & COCKTAIL PAIRINGS

WITH WATER?

☐ YES   ☐ NO

WITH ICE?

☐ YES   ☐ NO

LABEL/NOTES

NAME

PRODUCER

AGE

TYPE (bourbon, single malt Scotch, etc.)

GRAINS

☐ CORN   ☐ RYE

DESCRIPTIONS

COLOR

AROMA

TASTE

MOUTH-FEEL

TEXTURE

BALANCE

LENGTH

When?

Where?

Who with?

FOOD & COCKTAIL PAIRINGS

With water?

☐ Yes   ☐ No

With ice?

☐ Yes   ☐ No

Label/Notes

NAME

PRODUCER

AGE

TYPE (bourbon, single malt Scotch, etc.)

GRAINS

☐ CORN ☐ RYE

DESCRIPTIONS

COLOR

AROMA

TASTE

MOUTH-FEEL

TEXTURE

BALANCE

LENGTH

When?

Where?

Who with?

FOOD & COCKTAIL PAIRINGS

With water?

☐ Yes ☐ No

With ice?

☐ Yes ☐ No

Label/Notes

NAME

PRODUCER

AGE

TYPE (bourbon, single malt Scotch, etc.)

GRAINS

☐ CORN ☐ RYE

DESCRIPTIONS

COLOR

AROMA

TASTE

MOUTH-FEEL

TEXTURE

BALANCE

LENGTH

WHEN?

WHERE?

WHO WITH?

FOOD & COCKTAIL PAIRINGS

WITH WATER?

☐ YES   ☐ NO

WITH ICE?

☐ YES   ☐ NO

LABEL/NOTES

NAME

PRODUCER	AGE

TYPE (bourbon, single malt Scotch, etc.)	GRAINS
	□ CORN □ RYE

DESCRIPTIONS

COLOR	AROMA

TASTE	MOUTH-FEEL

TEXTURE

BALANCE

LENGTH

WHEN?

WHERE?

WHO WITH?

FOOD & COCKTAIL PAIRINGS

WITH WATER?

☐ YES   ☐ NO

WITH ICE?

☐ YES   ☐ NO

LABEL/NOTES

NAME

PRODUCER	AGE

TYPE (bourbon, single malt Scotch, etc.)	GRAINS
	☐ CORN ☐ RYE

DESCRIPTIONS

COLOR	AROMA

TASTE	MOUTH-FEEL

TEXTURE

BALANCE

LENGTH

When?

Where?

Who with?

FOOD & COCKTAIL PAIRINGS

With water?

☐ Yes ☐ No

With ice?

☐ Yes ☐ No

Label/Notes

NAME

PRODUCER	AGE
TYPE (bourbon, single malt Scotch, etc.)	GRAINS ☐ CORN ☐ RYE

DESCRIPTIONS

COLOR	AROMA
TASTE	MOUTH-FEEL

TEXTURE

BALANCE

LENGTH

WHEN?

WHERE?

WHO WITH?

FOOD & COCKTAIL PAIRINGS

WITH WATER?

☐ YES   ☐ NO

WITH ICE?

☐ YES   ☐ NO

LABEL/NOTES

NAME

PRODUCER

AGE

TYPE (bourbon, single malt Scotch, etc.)

GRAINS

☐ CORN ☐ RYE

DESCRIPTIONS

COLOR

AROMA

TASTE

MOUTH-FEEL

TEXTURE

BALANCE

LENGTH

WHEN?

WHERE?

WHO WITH?

FOOD & COCKTAIL PAIRINGS

WITH WATER?

☐ YES ☐ NO

WITH ICE?

☐ YES ☐ NO

LABEL/NOTES

NAME

PRODUCER | AGE

TYPE (bourbon, single malt Scotch, etc.) | GRAINS

☐ CORN ☐ RYE

DESCRIPTIONS

COLOR | AROMA

TASTE | MOUTH-FEEL

TEXTURE

BALANCE

LENGTH

WHEN?

WHERE?

WHO WITH?

FOOD & COCKTAIL PAIRINGS

WITH WATER?

☐ YES   ☐ NO

WITH ICE?

☐ YES   ☐ NO

LABEL/NOTES

NAME

PRODUCER	AGE

TYPE (bourbon, single malt Scotch, etc.)	GRAINS
	☐ CORN ☐ RYE

DESCRIPTIONS

COLOR	AROMA

TASTE	MOUTH-FEEL

TEXTURE

BALANCE

LENGTH

WHEN?

WHERE?

WHO WITH?

FOOD & COCKTAIL PAIRINGS

WITH WATER?	WITH ICE?
☐ YES ☐ NO	☐ YES ☐ NO

LABEL/NOTES

NAME

PRODUCER

AGE

TYPE (bourbon, single malt Scotch, etc.)

GRAINS

□ CORN   □ RYE

DESCRIPTIONS

COLOR

AROMA

TASTE

MOUTH-FEEL

TEXTURE

BALANCE

LENGTH

When?

Where?

Who with?

FOOD & COCKTAIL PAIRINGS

With water?

☐ Yes   ☐ No

With ice?

☐ Yes   ☐ No

Label/Notes

NAME

PRODUCER

AGE

TYPE (bourbon, single malt Scotch, etc.)

GRAINS

☐ CORN   ☐ RYE

DESCRIPTIONS

COLOR

AROMA

TASTE

MOUTH-FEEL

TEXTURE

BALANCE

LENGTH

WHEN?

WHERE?

WHO WITH?

FOOD & COCKTAIL PAIRINGS

WITH WATER?

☐ YES   ☐ NO

WITH ICE?

☐ YES   ☐ NO

LABEL/NOTES

NAME

PRODUCER	AGE

TYPE (bourbon, single malt Scotch, etc.)	GRAINS
	☐ CORN ☐ RYE

DESCRIPTIONS

COLOR	AROMA

TASTE	MOUTH-FEEL

TEXTURE

BALANCE

LENGTH

WHEN?

WHERE?

WHO WITH?

FOOD & COCKTAIL PAIRINGS

WITH WATER?

☐ YES   ☐ NO

WITH ICE?

☐ YES   ☐ NO

LABEL/NOTES

NAME

PRODUCER

AGE

TYPE (bourbon, single malt Scotch, etc.)

GRAINS

☐ CORN   ☐ RYE

DESCRIPTIONS

COLOR

AROMA

TASTE

MOUTH-FEEL

TEXTURE

BALANCE

LENGTH

When?

Where?

Who with?

FOOD & COCKTAIL PAIRINGS

With water?

☐ Yes   ☐ No

With ice?

☐ Yes   ☐ No

Label/Notes

NAME

PRODUCER | AGE

TYPE (bourbon, single malt Scotch, etc.) | GRAINS

☐ CORN ☐ RYE

DESCRIPTIONS

COLOR | AROMA

TASTE | MOUTH-FEEL

TEXTURE

BALANCE

LENGTH

WHEN?

WHERE?

WHO WITH?

FOOD & COCKTAIL PAIRINGS

WITH WATER?

□ YES   □ NO

WITH ICE?

□ YES   □ NO

LABEL/NOTES

NAME

PRODUCER | AGE

TYPE (bourbon, single malt Scotch, etc.) | GRAINS

☐ CORN ☐ RYE

DESCRIPTIONS

COLOR | AROMA

TASTE | MOUTH-FEEL

TEXTURE

BALANCE

LENGTH

When?

Where?

Who with?

FOOD & COCKTAIL PAIRINGS

With water?

☐ Yes   ☐ No

With ice?

☐ Yes   ☐ No

Label/Notes

NAME

PRODUCER

AGE

TYPE (bourbon, single malt Scotch, etc.)

GRAINS

☐ CORN ☐ RYE

DESCRIPTIONS

COLOR

AROMA

TASTE

MOUTH-FEEL

TEXTURE

BALANCE

LENGTH

When?

Where?

Who with?

FOOD & COCKTAIL PAIRINGS

With water?

☐ Yes ☐ No

With ice?

☐ Yes ☐ No

Label/Notes

NAME

PRODUCER	AGE

TYPE (bourbon, single malt Scotch, etc.)	GRAINS
	☐ CORN ☐ RYE

DESCRIPTIONS

COLOR	AROMA

TASTE	MOUTH-FEEL

TEXTURE

BALANCE

LENGTH

WHEN?

WHERE?

WHO WITH?

FOOD & COCKTAIL PAIRINGS

WITH WATER?

☐ YES   ☐ NO

WITH ICE?

☐ YES   ☐ NO

LABEL/NOTES

NAME

PRODUCER

AGE

TYPE (bourbon, single malt Scotch, etc.)

GRAINS

☐ CORN   ☐ RYE

DESCRIPTIONS

COLOR

AROMA

TASTE

MOUTH-FEEL

TEXTURE

BALANCE

LENGTH

WHEN?

WHERE?

WHO WITH?

FOOD & COCKTAIL PAIRINGS

WITH WATER?

☐ YES   ☐ NO

WITH ICE?

☐ YES   ☐ NO

LABEL/NOTES

NAME

PRODUCER | AGE

TYPE (bourbon, single malt Scotch, etc.) | GRAINS

☐ CORN   ☐ RYE

DESCRIPTIONS

COLOR | AROMA

TASTE | MOUTH-FEEL

TEXTURE

BALANCE

LENGTH

WHEN?

WHERE?

WHO WITH?

FOOD & COCKTAIL PAIRINGS

WITH WATER?

☐ YES   ☐ NO

WITH ICE?

☐ YES   ☐ NO

LABEL/NOTES

NAME

PRODUCER

AGE

TYPE (bourbon, single malt Scotch, etc.)

GRAINS

☐ CORN   ☐ RYE

DESCRIPTIONS

COLOR

AROMA

TASTE

MOUTH-FEEL

TEXTURE

BALANCE

LENGTH

WHEN?

WHERE?

WHO WITH?

FOOD & COCKTAIL PAIRINGS

WITH WATER?

☐ Yes ☐ No

WITH ICE?

☐ Yes ☐ No

LABEL/NOTES

NAME

PRODUCER | AGE

TYPE (bourbon, single malt Scotch, etc.) | GRAINS

☐ CORN ☐ RYE

DESCRIPTIONS

COLOR | AROMA

TASTE | MOUTH-FEEL

TEXTURE

BALANCE

LENGTH

WHEN?

WHERE?

WHO WITH?

FOOD & COCKTAIL PAIRINGS

WITH WATER?

☐ YES   ☐ NO

WITH ICE?

☐ YES   ☐ NO

LABEL/NOTES

NAME

PRODUCER

AGE

TYPE (bourbon, single malt Scotch, etc.)

GRAINS

☐ CORN ☐ RYE

DESCRIPTIONS

COLOR

AROMA

TASTE

MOUTH-FEEL

TEXTURE

BALANCE

LENGTH

WHEN?

WHERE?

WHO WITH?

FOOD & COCKTAIL PAIRINGS

WITH WATER?

☐ YES   ☐ NO

WITH ICE?

☐ YES   ☐ NO

LABEL/NOTES

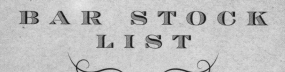

BAR STOCK
LIST

Good news, bad news. You just wowed your friends with a great bottle of Scotch, but you can't remember where you got it. Or, you want to pair your dinner with that perfect bourbon with a hint of caramel, but you don't remember which one that was, and you don't want to have to taste them all (not before the guest arrive, anyway). Make it easy on yourself by keeping track of what you stock in your bar. And of course, there's nothing more fun that recording your bar stock, then offering up the list to friends with your notes to let them choose what they'd like on sip.

NAME

DATE PURCHASED | AGE

TYPE (bourbon, single malt Scotch, etc.)

GRAINS

☐ CORN   ☐ RYE   ☐ BARLEY   ☐ WHEAT   ☐ OTHER

BAR STOCK LIST

NAME

DATE PURCHASED | AGE

TYPE (bourbon, single malt Scotch, etc.)

GRAINS

☐ CORN   ☐ RYE   ☐ BARLEY   ☐ WHEAT   ☐ OTHER

NAME

DATE PURCHASED | AGE

TYPE (bourbon, single malt Scotch, etc.)

GRAINS

☐ CORN ☐ RYE ☐ BARLEY ☐ WHEAT ☐ OTHER

BAR STOCK LIST

NAME

DATE PURCHASED | AGE

TYPE (bourbon, single malt Scotch, etc.)

GRAINS

☐ CORN ☐ RYE ☐ BARLEY ☐ WHEAT ☐ OTHER

NAME

DATE PURCHASED | AGE

TYPE (bourbon, single malt Scotch, etc.)

GRAINS

☐ CORN ☐ RYE ☐ BARLEY ☐ WHEAT ☐ OTHER

BAR STOCK LIST

NAME

DATE PURCHASED | AGE

TYPE (bourbon, single malt Scotch, etc.)

GRAINS

☐ CORN ☐ RYE ☐ BARLEY ☐ WHEAT ☐ OTHER

NAME

DATE PURCHASED | AGE

TYPE (bourbon, single malt Scotch, etc.)

GRAINS

☐ CORN   ☐ RYE   ☐ BARLEY   ☐ WHEAT   ☐ OTHER

BAR STOCK LIST

NAME

DATE PURCHASED | AGE

TYPE (bourbon, single malt Scotch, etc.)

GRAINS

☐ CORN   ☐ RYE   ☐ BARLEY   ☐ WHEAT   ☐ OTHER

NAME

DATE PURCHASED | AGE

TYPE (bourbon, single malt Scotch, etc.)

GRAINS

☐ CORN ☐ RYE ☐ BARLEY ☐ WHEAT ☐ OTHER

BAR STOCK LIST

NAME

DATE PURCHASED | AGE

TYPE (bourbon, single malt Scotch, etc.)

GRAINS

☐ CORN ☐ RYE ☐ BARLEY ☐ WHEAT ☐ OTHER

NAME

DATE PURCHASED | AGE

TYPE (bourbon, single malt Scotch, etc.)

GRAINS

☐ CORN   ☐ RYE   ☐ BARLEY   ☐ WHEAT   ☐ OTHER

BAR STOCK LIST

NAME

DATE PURCHASED | AGE

TYPE (bourbon, single malt Scotch, etc.)

GRAINS

☐ CORN   ☐ RYE   ☐ BARLEY   ☐ WHEAT   ☐ OTHER

NAME

DATE PURCHASED | AGE

TYPE (bourbon, single malt Scotch, etc.)

GRAINS

☐ CORN ☐ RYE ☐ BARLEY ☐ WHEAT ☐ OTHER

BAR STOCK LIST

NAME

DATE PURCHASED | AGE

TYPE (bourbon, single malt Scotch, etc.)

GRAINS

☐ CORN ☐ RYE ☐ BARLEY ☐ WHEAT ☐ OTHER

NAME

DATE PURCHASED | AGE

TYPE (bourbon, single malt Scotch, etc.)

GRAINS

☐ CORN   ☐ RYE   ☐ BARLEY   ☐ WHEAT   ☐ OTHER

BAR STOCK LIST

NAME

DATE PURCHASED | AGE

TYPE (bourbon, single malt Scotch, etc.)

GRAINS

☐ CORN   ☐ RYE   ☐ BARLEY   ☐ WHEAT   ☐ OTHER

NAME

DATE PURCHASED | AGE

TYPE (bourbon, single malt Scotch, etc.)

GRAINS

☐ CORN   ☐ RYE   ☐ BARLEY   ☐ WHEAT   ☐ OTHER

BAR STOCK LIST

NAME

DATE PURCHASED | AGE

TYPE (bourbon, single malt Scotch, etc.)

GRAINS

☐ CORN   ☐ RYE   ☐ BARLEY   ☐ WHEAT   ☐ OTHER

NAME

DATE PURCHASED | AGE

TYPE (bourbon, single malt Scotch, etc.)

GRAINS

☐ CORN   ☐ RYE   ☐ BARLEY   ☐ WHEAT   ☐ OTHER

BAR STOCK LIST

NAME

DATE PURCHASED | AGE

TYPE (bourbon, single malt Scotch, etc.)

GRAINS

☐ CORN   ☐ RYE   ☐ BARLEY   ☐ WHEAT   ☐ OTHER

NAME

DATE PURCHASED | AGE

TYPE (bourbon, single malt Scotch, etc.)

GRAINS

☐ CORN ☐ RYE ☐ BARLEY ☐ WHEAT ☐ OTHER

BAR STOCK LIST

NAME

DATE PURCHASED | AGE

TYPE (bourbon, single malt Scotch, etc.)

GRAINS

☐ CORN ☐ RYE ☐ BARLEY ☐ WHEAT ☐ OTHER

NAME

DATE PURCHASED | AGE

TYPE (bourbon, single malt Scotch, etc.)

GRAINS

☐ CORN   ☐ RYE   ☐ BARLEY   ☐ WHEAT   ☐ OTHER

BAR STOCK LIST

NAME

DATE PURCHASED | AGE

TYPE (bourbon, single malt Scotch, etc.)

GRAINS

☐ CORN   ☐ RYE   ☐ BARLEY   ☐ WHEAT   ☐ OTHER

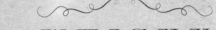

WHISKY
SHORT LIST

You had a great time. Great whisky. Great company. Fabulous food. Old-school bar setting. You just want to get down on paper the most memorable parts, and you want to make sure you remember that bottle of whisky so you can drink it again! Well, here's your chance. You don't always need to be long-winded. Sometimes just remarking on what you wanted to remember about it is enough, so feel free to leave whatever spaces you want blank. Be concise where you want to be and thorough where it matters to you!

NAME	DATE

DATE PURCHASED	AGE

TYPE (bourbon, single malt Scotch, etc.)

GRAINS

☐ CORN   ☐ RYE   ☐ BARLEY   ☐ WHEAT   ☐ OTHER

PLACE PURCHASED

WHO WITH?	PRICE

DESCRIPTION | NOTES

NAME	DATE

DATE PURCHASED	AGE

TYPE (bourbon, single malt Scotch, etc.)

GRAINS

☐ CORN   ☐ RYE   ☐ BARLEY   ☐ WHEAT   ☐ OTHER

PLACE PURCHASED

WHO WITH?	PRICE

DESCRIPTION | NOTES

NAME

DATE

DATE PURCHASED

AGE

TYPE (bourbon, single malt Scotch, etc.)

GRAINS

☐ CORN   ☐ RYE   ☐ BARLEY   ☐ WHEAT   ☐ OTHER

PLACE PURCHASED

WHO WITH?

PRICE

DESCRIPTION | NOTES

NAME

DATE

DATE PURCHASED

AGE

TYPE (bourbon, single malt Scotch, etc.)

GRAINS

☐ CORN   ☐ RYE   ☐ BARLEY   ☐ WHEAT   ☐ OTHER

PLACE PURCHASED

WHO WITH?

PRICE

DESCRIPTION | NOTES

NAME

DATE

DATE PURCHASED

AGE

TYPE (bourbon, single malt Scotch, etc.)

GRAINS

☐ CORN   ☐ RYE   ☐ BARLEY   ☐ WHEAT   ☐ OTHER

PLACE PURCHASED

WHO WITH?

PRICE

DESCRIPTION | NOTES

NAME	DATE

DATE PURCHASED	AGE

TYPE (bourbon, single malt Scotch, etc.)

GRAINS

☐ CORN ☐ RYE ☐ BARLEY ☐ WHEAT ☐ OTHER

PLACE PURCHASED

WHO WITH?	PRICE

DESCRIPTION | NOTES

NAME

DATE

DATE PURCHASED

AGE

TYPE (bourbon, single malt Scotch, etc.)

GRAINS

☐ CORN   ☐ RYE   ☐ BARLEY   ☐ WHEAT   ☐ OTHER

PLACE PURCHASED

WHO WITH?

PRICE

DESCRIPTION | NOTES

NAME	DATE
DATE PURCHASED	AGE

TYPE (bourbon, single malt Scotch, etc.)

GRAINS

☐ CORN   ☐ RYE   ☐ BARLEY   ☐ WHEAT   ☐ OTHER

PLACE PURCHASED

WHO WITH?	PRICE

DESCRIPTION | NOTES

NAME	DATE

DATE PURCHASED	AGE

TYPE (bourbon, single malt Scotch, etc.)

GRAINS

☐ CORN   ☐ RYE   ☐ BARLEY   ☐ WHEAT   ☐ OTHER

PLACE PURCHASED

WHO WITH?	PRICE

DESCRIPTION | NOTES

NAME	DATE
DATE PURCHASED	AGE

TYPE (bourbon, single malt Scotch, etc.)

GRAINS

☐ CORN   ☐ RYE   ☐ BARLEY   ☐ WHEAT   ☐ OTHER

PLACE PURCHASED

WHO WITH?	PRICE

DESCRIPTION | NOTES

NAME	DATE

DATE PURCHASED	AGE

TYPE (bourbon, single malt Scotch, etc.)

GRAINS

☐ CORN   ☐ RYE   ☐ BARLEY   ☐ WHEAT   ☐ OTHER

PLACE PURCHASED

WHO WITH?	PRICE

DESCRIPTION | NOTES

NAME

DATE

DATE PURCHASED

AGE

TYPE (bourbon, single malt Scotch, etc.)

GRAINS

☐ CORN   ☐ RYE   ☐ BARLEY   ☐ WHEAT   ☐ OTHER

PLACE PURCHASED

WHO WITH?

PRICE

DESCRIPTION | NOTES

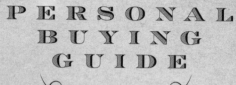

PERSONAL BUYING GUIDE

If you're like most whisky drinkers, you don't buy your whisky exclusively at one store. (Maybe you even buy it online.) You don't always buy the same type, and sometimes you just go with the one that looks cool. That's the fun of drinking whisky! But to make sure you remember all your favorites as you expand your whisky horizons, following are some pages for you to write down each of your favorites types. Then, record your favorite shops (along with their vital info) so you remember where to return again and again. Getting to know the people who work at your local spirits shop can lead to fantastic recommendations, personal tastings, and more.

All-Time Favorites

Favorite Ryes

Favorite Bourbons

Favorite Corn Whiskies

Favorite Single Malt Scotches

Favorite Blended Scotches

Favorite Single Grain Whiskies

Other Favorites

SHOP NAME

ADDRESS/PHONE/EMAIL

WEBSITE/SOCIAL MEDIA	BEST BUYS

NOTES

◆§ SHOP PAGES §◆

SHOP NAME

LOCATION/ADDRESS	PHONE

WEBSITE/SOCIAL MEDIA	BEST BUYS

NOTES

SHOP NAME

ADDRESS/PHONE/EMAIL

WEBSITE/SOCIAL MEDIA	BEST BUYS

NOTES

❧ SHOP PAGES ☙

SHOP NAME

LOCATION/ADDRESS	PHONE

WEBSITE/SOCIAL MEDIA	BEST BUYS

NOTES

SHOP NAME

ADDRESS/PHONE/EMAIL

WEBSITE/SOCIAL MEDIA	BEST BUYS

NOTES

◆ᘓ SHOP PAGES ᘔ◆

SHOP NAME

LOCATION/ADDRESS	PHONE

WEBSITE/SOCIAL MEDIA	BEST BUYS

NOTES

SHOP NAME

ADDRESS/PHONE/EMAIL

WEBSITE/SOCIAL MEDIA	BEST BUYS

NOTES

SHOP PAGES

SHOP NAME

LOCATION/ADDRESS	PHONE

WEBSITE/SOCIAL MEDIA	BEST BUYS

NOTES

SHOP NAME

ADDRESS/PHONE/EMAIL

WEBSITE/SOCIAL MEDIA | BEST BUYS

NOTES

◆⟨ **SHOP PAGES** ⟩◆

SHOP NAME

LOCATION/ADDRESS | PHONE

WEBSITE/SOCIAL MEDIA | BEST BUYS

NOTES

Shop Name

Address/Phone/Email

Website/Social Media	Best Buys

Notes

$\cdot\xi$ SHOP PAGES $\xi\cdot$

Shop Name

Location/Address	Phone

Website/Social Media	Best Buys

Notes

SHOP NAME

ADDRESS/PHONE/EMAIL

WEBSITE/SOCIAL MEDIA	BEST BUYS

NOTES

◆⦃ SHOP PAGES ⦄◆

SHOP NAME

LOCATION/ADDRESS	PHONE

WEBSITE/SOCIAL MEDIA	BEST BUYS

NOTES

SHOP NAME

ADDRESS/PHONE/EMAIL

WEBSITE/SOCIAL MEDIA | BEST BUYS

NOTES

SHOP PAGES

SHOP NAME

LOCATION/ADDRESS | PHONE

WEBSITE/SOCIAL MEDIA | BEST BUYS

NOTES

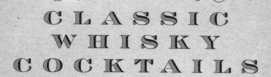

CLASSIC
WHISKY
COCKTAILS

There are today numerous whisky cocktails. Hundreds of them seemingly pop up every day, especially with the proliferation of craft spirits. Herein is a list of ten of history's classic whisky cocktails. Many of these have been staples at bars throughout North America for more than a century. The original ingredients are listed, but you can substitute whiskies as you try new ones and collect them.

OLD FASHIONED

The Old Fashioned is arguably among the oldest cocktails recipes—if not the oldest—in the great canon of cocktails. Some citations date it back as far as 1806.

1 sugar cube
2 dashes Angostura bitters
1 orange slice
1 Maraschino cherry
1 jigger whisky
Few dashes still water

In a whisky glass, dissolve sugar cube. Add bitters. Add orange slice and maraschino cherry. Using a muddler, crush the sugar, the fruit, and the bitters together well. Now, add whisky. Mix with small bar spoon. Serve.

MANHATTAN

The Manhattan is a storied drink, with more than a few apocryphal origins. Suffice to say, it was invented in the mid- to late-1800s, most likely by a bartender named Black in a bar in Manhattan, New York City, on Broadway near Houston Street. Some drinkers prefer dry vermouth.

1 jigger American rye
  or Canadian whisky
1 shot sweet red vermouth
1 dash Angostura bitters
  Ice cubes, to
    fill cocktail shaker
1 Maraschino cherry

Add whisky, vermouth, and bitters to a cocktail shaker filled with ice. Stir vigorously. Strain into a chilled cocktail glass. Add Maraschino cherry for garnish. Serve.

ROB ROY

The Rob Roy is a cocktail created in 1894 by a bartender at the Waldorf Astoria in Manhattan, New York City. The drink was named in honor of the Scottish folk hero Robert

1 jigger Scotch whisky
1 shot sweet vermouth
1 dash Angostura bitters
2-3 ice cubes

Roy MacGregor. Appropriately, the bartender insisted on using Scotch whisky. A Rob Roy may be ordered "straight up" or "on the rocks" depending on the drinker's preference. Also, some drinkers prefer dry vermouth.

In a shaker add whisky, vermouth, and bitters over ice. Stir. Strain into chilled cocktail or Martini glass, or pour over ice for "on the rocks."

SAZERAC

The Sazerac is a local New Orleans variation of a Cognac or whisky cocktail. It is the official cocktail of New Orleans. The drink was named for the Sazerac de Forge et Fils brand of Cognac which was the original main ingredient. The cocktail is among one of the older classic American cocktail recipes, although it is highly doubtful it is the oldest. A classic Sazerac is made with cognac, but a whisky variation was common back in the day, most likely with American rye. The distinctive idea behind a Sazerac is its preparation.

1 shot absinthe
2-3 crushed ice cubes
1 jigger whisky or Cognac
1 sugar cube
2 dashes Peychaud's Bitters
1 lemon peel

Rinse a chilled old-fashioned glass with absinthe. Add crushed ice and then set glass aside. In a shaker, over ice, add whisky (or Cognac), sugar, and bitters. Stir. Discard the ice and absinthe from the prepared glass, and strain the drink into the glass. Add lemon peel for garnish.

BROOKLYN

This Prohibition-era drink is a variation of the Manhattan. The thing about a Brooklyn is that it calls for American rye, and it uses different bitters and flavoring agents. A fun cocktail that disappeared for a while, but made its comeback more than 20 years ago, it is now considered a classic.

1 jigger American rye or Canadian whisky
1 shot dry vermouth
¼ oz Maraschino liqueur
¼ oz Amer Picon or a few dashes of Angostura bitters
2-3 ice cubes
1 Maraschino cherry

Mix whisky, vermouth, liqueur, and bitters in a shaker over ice. Stir. Strain into chilled cocktail glass. Add Maraschino cherry for garnish.

WHISKY SOUR

The whisky sour, sometimes referred to as a Boston Sour, dates back to the 1870s; the first mention anyone can find of it is in an 1870 Wisconsin newspaper clipping. It is credited to Elliott Stubb, who supposedly created the "whisky sour" in 1872. The drink is made with egg whites, which give it a frothy head, but substitutes may be found for those who do not wish to use egg products. Commercial substitutes or pineapple juice may be used.

In a cocktail shaker combine whisky, juice, syrup, and egg white (or other frothing agent). Shake vigorously. Pour into a whisky glass filled with fresh ice. Add maraschino cherry (or lemon or orange slice), for garnish.

1 jigger Bourbon whisky
1 shot fresh lemon juice
1 shot Gomme syrup
1 dash egg white (or other frothing agent)
  Ice cubes, to fill whisky glass
1 Maraschino cherry (or lemon or orange slice)

RUSTY NAIL

The drink first appeared in 1937, probably in Britain. The name Rusty Nail was established by bartenders at the 21 Club in the 1960s. It was also made popular as a favorite drink of the Rat Pack. In the upper Midwest, this recipe is referred to as a Knucklehead.

1 jigger Scotch Whisky
1 shot Drambuie
  Ice cubes, to fill whisky glass
1 lemon twist

Mix the whisky and Drambuie in a whisky glass filled with ice. Stir gently. Garnish with a lemon twist.

SUBURBAN

According to numerous sources, this cocktail was created in the mid-1880s, and named for the Suburban Handicap, a thoroughbred horse race. The Suburban Handicap (held on Long Island) was the last of the three races that formed the New York Handicap Triple (a New York version of today's Triple Crown).

  Ice cubes, to fill cocktail shaker
1 jigger rye whisky
½ **shot** port wine
½ **shot** dark rum
3 dashes orange bitters
3 dashes Angostura bitters

In a shaker filled with ice, add whisky, wine, rum, and bitters. Shake vigorously. Strain into a cocktail or Martini glass.

BLOOD AND SAND

Blood and Sand was originally named for Rudolph Valentino's 1922 bullfighter movie *Blood and Sand* (which was remade in 1941 with Tyrone Power, Linda Darnell, and Rita Hayworth). The recipe first appeared in the 1930 classic compendium *Savoy Cocktail Book*.

Ice cubes, to fill cocktail shaker
1 shot whisky
1 shot blood orange juice
1 shot sweet vermouth
1 shot Cherry Heering
1 orange slice or dash orange zest

In a cocktail shaker filled with ice, mix the whisky, juice, vermouth, and Cherry Heering. Shake vigorously. Strain into cocktail or Martini glass. Add orange slice or a dash of orange zest to garnish.

GLASGOW

This cocktail is named for the Scottish city and was originally made with Scotch whisky. Today, it has numerous variations. But it is considered among the classics of whisky cocktails, and an odd-ball favorite among the mixologist elite.

1 jigger whisky
1 shot dry vermouth
1 teaspoon lemon juice
1 dash Peychaud's Bitters
Ice cubes, to fill cocktail shaker
1 lemon twist

Combine whisky, vermouth, lemon juice, and bitters in a shaker full of ice. Stir vigorously. Strain and pour into a cocktail or Martini glass. Add lemon twist for garnish.

COCKTAIL RECIPES

There is nothing more fun than going to a bar or a friend's house and finding a new cocktail recipe you like. With all the new craft whiskies, as well as the classic standbys, and with all that's going on in the cocktail world, there's never been a better time to try new things, and even experiment yourself!

Here's an easy, simple section of cocktail recipe pages for you to fill out when you find a few more that catch your fancy!

DRINK NAME:

INGREDIENTS:

AMOUNT   NAME

_____   _____

_____   _____

_____   _____

_____   _____

_____   _____

_____   _____

INSTRUCTIONS:

_____

_____

_____

_____

GARNISH WITH? _____

_____

DRINK NAME:

INGREDIENTS:

AMOUNT	NAME
_____	_____
_____	_____
_____	_____
_____	_____
_____	_____
_____	_____

INSTRUCTIONS:

_____

_____

_____

_____

GARNISH WITH? _____

_____

DRINK NAME:

INGREDIENTS:

AMOUNT	NAME
_____	_____
_____	_____
_____	_____
_____	_____
_____	_____
_____	_____

INSTRUCTIONS:

_____

_____

_____

_____

GARNISH WITH? _____

_____

DRINK NAME:

INGREDIENTS:

AMOUNT	NAME
_____	_____
_____	_____
_____	_____
_____	_____
_____	_____

INSTRUCTIONS:

_____

_____

_____

_____

GARNISH WITH? _____

DRINK NAME:

INGREDIENTS:

AMOUNT	NAME
_____	_____
_____	_____
_____	_____
_____	_____
_____	_____

INSTRUCTIONS:

_____

_____

_____

_____

GARNISH WITH? _____

DRINK NAME:

INGREDIENTS:

AMOUNT	NAME
_____	_____
_____	_____
_____	_____
_____	_____
_____	_____
_____	_____

INSTRUCTIONS:

_____
_____
_____
_____

GARNISH WITH? _____
_____

DRINK NAME:

INGREDIENTS:

AMOUNT	NAME
_____	_____
_____	_____
_____	_____
_____	_____
_____	_____
_____	_____

INSTRUCTIONS:

_____
_____
_____
_____

GARNISH WITH? _____
_____

DRINK NAME:

INGREDIENTS:

AMOUNT   NAME

_____   _____

_____   _____

_____   _____

_____   _____

_____   _____

_____   _____

INSTRUCTIONS:

_____

_____

_____

_____

GARNISH WITH? _____

_____

DRINK NAME:

INGREDIENTS:

AMOUNT   NAME

_____   _____

_____   _____

_____   _____

_____   _____

_____   _____

_____   _____

INSTRUCTIONS:

_____

_____

_____

_____

GARNISH WITH? _____

_____

DRINK NAME:

INGREDIENTS:

AMOUNT	NAME
_____	_____
_____	_____
_____	_____
_____	_____
_____	_____
_____	_____

INSTRUCTIONS:

_____

_____

_____

_____

GARNISH WITH? _____

_____

DRINK NAME:

INGREDIENTS:

AMOUNT	NAME
_____	_____
_____	_____
_____	_____
_____	_____
_____	_____
_____	_____

INSTRUCTIONS:

_____

_____

_____

_____

GARNISH WITH? _____

_____

DRINK NAME:

INGREDIENTS:

AMOUNT	NAME

INSTRUCTIONS:

GARNISH WITH? _____

DRINK NAME:

INGREDIENTS:

AMOUNT	NAME

INSTRUCTIONS:

GARNISH WITH? _____

DRINK NAME:

INGREDIENTS:

AMOUNT	NAME
_____	_____
_____	_____
_____	_____
_____	_____
_____	_____
_____	_____

INSTRUCTIONS:

_____

_____

_____

_____

GARNISH WITH? _____

_____

DRINK NAME:

INGREDIENTS:

AMOUNT	NAME
_____	_____
_____	_____
_____	_____
_____	_____
_____	_____
_____	_____

INSTRUCTIONS:

_____

_____

_____

_____

GARNISH WITH? _____

_____

DRINK NAME:

INGREDIENTS:

AMOUNT	NAME
_____	_____
_____	_____
_____	_____
_____	_____
_____	_____

INSTRUCTIONS:

_____

_____

_____

_____

GARNISH WITH? _____

_____

DRINK NAME:

INGREDIENTS:

AMOUNT	NAME
_____	_____
_____	_____
_____	_____
_____	_____
_____	_____

INSTRUCTIONS:

_____

_____

_____

_____

GARNISH WITH? _____

_____

DRINK NAME:

INGREDIENTS:

AMOUNT	NAME
_____	_____
_____	_____
_____	_____
_____	_____
_____	_____
_____	_____

INSTRUCTIONS:

_____

_____

_____

_____

GARNISH WITH? _____

_____

DRINK NAME:

INGREDIENTS:

AMOUNT	NAME
_____	_____
_____	_____
_____	_____
_____	_____
_____	_____
_____	_____

INSTRUCTIONS:

_____

_____

_____

_____

GARNISH WITH? _____

_____

DRINK NAME:

INGREDIENTS:

AMOUNT	NAME

INSTRUCTIONS:

GARNISH WITH? _____

DRINK NAME:

INGREDIENTS:

AMOUNT	NAME

INSTRUCTIONS:

GARNISH WITH? _____

DRINK NAME:

INGREDIENTS:

AMOUNT	NAME
_____	_____
_____	_____
_____	_____
_____	_____
_____	_____

INSTRUCTIONS:

_____

_____

_____

_____

GARNISH WITH? _____

_____

DRINK NAME:

INGREDIENTS:

AMOUNT	NAME
_____	_____
_____	_____
_____	_____
_____	_____
_____	_____

INSTRUCTIONS:

_____

_____

_____

_____

GARNISH WITH? _____

_____

GLOSSARY

Alcohol by volume (ABV): The amount of alcohol as a percentage of the total volume. The higher the number, the stronger the whisky.

Angel's Share: The amount of whisky that evaporates during barrel aging.

Austere: Straightforward, little else.

Balanced: A good blend of aromas and flavors resulting in a complex, well-made whisky.

Big: Bold, in your face, dominates the mouth.

Body: How your mouth feels the liquid. Is it thin? Watery? Big? Spicy? Luxurious?

Cask: A large wooden barrel, usually oak, that whisky is aged in.

Cask strength: The strength of whisky pulled straight from the cask. Usually between 40 percent and 65 percent ABV.

Cereal: Taste that reminds one of grains or grain foods, e.g., sweet corn, corn flakes, oatmeal, etc.

Charred: A barrel that has been burned to blackness on the inside. Especially used to make bourbon.

Chill filtration: When whisky is chilled to such a degree that it becomes cloudy and solids form and drop to the bottom of the water column, and then the liquid is filtered. Improves whisky clarity, quality, and stability.

Column still: A still used for commercial distillation. Column stills usually have one tall column, with portals on them so that the distiller can see the level in the column. Sometimes also called a Coffey still, or a continuous still.

Condensation: Process where alcohol vapors go through a cooling tube connected to the still and condense back into liquid.

Cooper: A highly skilled barrel maker.

Complex: A whisky that brings forth numerous layers of long-lasting aroma and taste, in balance. Each time one sips the liquid, another nuance of flavor is discovered.

Creamy: A smooth mouth-feel reminiscent of custard or half and half.

Dank: A smell like wet basement, wet matted leaves, wet hay, or wet grass.

Dark sugars: The whisky, either by aroma or taste, reminds one of caramel, butterscotch, toffee, or other similar burnt sugar flavors.

Dram: A traditional measure for serving whisky.

Dry: Lacking in sweetness of any kind. Leaves the mouth puckering.

Estery: Floral or flowery fruit smells in a whisky. Pineapple, apple, and banana are typical estery aromas.

Ethanol: When you can smell the alcohol in a whisky.

Finish: After you have savored the liquid, then swallowed, that lingering taste that remains in the mouth for the next 15–30 seconds.

Floral: Hints of violets, lavender, or honeysuckle.

Floor malting: Old-fashioned process of taking barley soaked in water and spreading it out on a floor to germinate. Must be regularly turned by hand in order to germinate properly. Very, very time consuming, only practiced by the best distilleries.

Legs: The streaks of liquid that linger on the insides of the glass after the liquid has been swirled around.

Mash: The mixture of grown grains and water that's used to make whisky.

Malting: In making whisky, the process of soaking the grain and then laying it out to dry. This allows it to germinate, and its starches to more easily convert to sugars.

Malty: This refers to the aromas and flavors of malt or malted barley.

Medicinal: A whisky that smells like rubbing alcohol and tastes like cough syrup.

Mouth-feel: The way the liquid feels in your mouth. Watery? Thin? Big? Flavorful? Aftertaste?

Nose: The aroma given off by the whiskey.

Peat: A brown mass of partly decomposed vegetable matter including grasses or even mosses used to power the kilns that heat barley as it's being malted. A "peaty" whisky is a whisky that tastes big and smoky with a peppery aftertaste. The really over-the-top ones are called "peat monsters."

Phenolic: Tar-like aromas that can sometimes take over alcoholic beverages. Generally thought of as a fault.

Pot still: Copper stills that are most commonly used in the production of single malt whisky.

Proof: An old English measure of alcohol in a product. Proof is exactly two times the ABV, e.g., 80 proof whisky has an ABV of 40 percent.

Sherry: Whisky that has the same aroma profiles of sherry, i.e. dark fruits, hazelnut, etc. A "sherried" whisky may have been aged in a sherry cask.

Vegetative: Reminds the taster of green grass, hay, or even green pepper.

Viscous: The thickness of the liquid. Some are watery thin, and others are more unctuous. A viscous whisky will have more legs.

Youthful: Full of vibrant, volatile, light characteristics. Flavors may not be well integrated. Think of a young wine.

Warm: Reminiscent of physical warmth, like freshly brewed tea.

Wort: The resulting liquid from cooked grains that contains the sugars necessary for fermentation.